How My Anal Fistula Healed Naturally

-No surgery, seton, or magical herbs

Penni X. W.

ISBN: 978-0-578-90779-6

DEDICATION

To Chris and Mei.

Disclaimer: The opinions expressed in this book are solely that of the author and are not intended to constitute any medical advice to anyone. Readers are warned to use this book at their own discretion.

CONTENTS

1. Preface

First of all, thank you for investing in this book and for supporting what I do for the "Rear Care" community!

If you are looking for an anal fistula natural healing story, as I was when first diagnosed, you've found the right place. I had an anal abscess diagnosed in May 2017, and a fistula diagnosed three months later. A fistulotomy, a surgery to remove the fistula, was presented to me as the only option. As my fistula was part of the complications from a hemorrhoidectomy (hemorrhoid removal surgery), I did not want another surgery. I wanted and needed a natural remedy instead.

At the time of the fistula diagnosis, I had been dealing with other anal complications for about 10 months since the "ill-fated" hemorrhoidectomy. I had done tons of research and developed a rigorous daily self-care regimen. My symptoms were largely under control despite severe challenges. Although the fistula diagnosis was devastating, I heard a little voice at the back of my head telling me I should tackle this one as I did with other complications. At least, I should try. Mentally, I was not ready for another surgery either.

Information on anal fistula natural healing was extremely limited. 99% of the information I found had indicated that a fistula cannot heal on its own. The first self-healing story I read about was a Chinese patient's recount of how he controlled his fistula symptoms with at home care. His story gave me enough confidence to believe that it's possible to at least control the fistula symptoms. I developed and added new steps to my daily self-care regimen, aiming to control the fistula symptoms. Although it took me some time to get a hang of the new steps, my body reacted positively - symptoms fluctuated at the beginning, and gradually subsided.

At a check-up, exactly a year after the fistula diagnosis, I told the colon rectal surgeon (CRS) that I did not have any drainage for a while. He used a probe to check the fistula tunnel and declared the tunnel had closed on its own. I had another check-up ten months later, the fistula remained closed.

Some might call my fistula "dormant". I guess only time will tell. Without any drainage, the CRS does not see a point to surgically cut out an asymptomatic and seemingly closed fistula. As far as I am concerned, the fistula has been gradually receding from my daily life. I do not think about it much nowadays. I obviously continue to use caution when it comes to diet and hygiene – these are healthy habits I want to keep anyway.

I hesitated to share my story because stories like this can be considered taboos or outlaws in the medical community, for a good reason – anal patients, who suffer enough already from excruciating pain and embarrassment, do not need untested, unfounded fantasies to further complicate and aggravate their pain.

Nevertheless, not telling my story also feels wrong as I believe anal patients are generally under-served in that anal illnesses are less discussed in public and patients are used to suffering in silence. The pain associated with anal diseases are impossible to relate to unless one actually experiences it. Anal illnesses, though not fatal (mostly), significantly impact one's daily life and mental health. Treatments in anal illness seem to remain stagnant for decades, while exciting new drugs and treatments pop up often in other areas.

I started my blog website www.rearcare.com to share my experience about battling complications from a hemorrhoidectomy, as well as participated on various patient forums. Sharing and learning had been a part of my healing.

Other people's healing stories always gave me hope. I wish my story of healing does the same to others. Although I may not have the most complicated fistula case, I believe what I have done can inspire many patients to control their symptoms and possibly heal as I have. With the help of friends and family, I wrote down my story. If this book can help inspire one patient to get better, all my effort in putting together this book will be worth it.

Regards,

Penni

Founder of RearCare.com

2. The Day Fistula Heals…

I think it is important to feel positive and hopeful in our healing, even if not all the time, at least sometime. It helps us feel better and stronger mentally. These positive vibes will convert into strength we need to fight against fistula. In my two and a half years battle against complications from the hemorrhoidectomy, I had countless occasions when my symptoms felt worse and I was so depleted and in pain. I also had severe panic attacks prior to all doctors 'visits, fearing for the pain during the exam and the bad news I wasn't ready to accept. I had made three appointments and cancelled them all due to anxiety. In spite of all of these, I always found hope again either from other patients 'positive posts or from my own body, which had bounced back after each and every obstacle. Despite all the fears and worries, I always kept a small space in my heart to fantasize that my fistula would heal one day.

Before I went to see a proctologist for a follow-up exactly one year after my fistula diagnosis, I hardly had any fistula symptoms any more. While I wanted to consider that I was healing, I was more worried the fistula was just as bad inside and possibly "branching around" fiercely without me knowing.

When the proctologist declared that my anal fistula closed on its own and I no longer needed surgery, I could not believe his words. I kept asking, "How is it possible? Wouldn't a fistula never heal on its own?" The doctor did not have a good answer. I didn't mind, either. After all, my abscess-turned-fistula, closed on its own without any surgical intervention!

To me, the small space of hope in my heart kept me fighting and enjoying life as much as I could. Its positive vibes were answered by the rest of my body.

I want to remind everyone, before reading my book, to find your inner strength and safeguard a small space in your heart to hope and prepare for the day your fistula will heal or become asymptomatic. Please remember, we are in this together.

3 Decoding Myth and Facts of Fistula

I never thought my healing was pure luck. In fact, my lucky score couldn't have been high given I had developed nearly all possible complications from a hemorrhoidectomy. I spent countless hours at studying fistula and other complications. I read medical papers, browsed through hundreds of discussion forums, followed social media groups and influencers, and also researched Chinese and Indian traditional treatments. I tried different approaches to facilitate my healing, some worked and some failed. It has been a journey of constant trials and errors.

For those inquisitive minds, this chapter will dig into what I've learned about fistula and how these understandings support my belief that natural healing is actually more likely than we had assumed, at least for many common fistulae that are routinely resolved by surgeries. For those of you who are in a hurry and just want to know how I did it, you can skip over to the next section directly.

Fistula is a scary and embarrassing condition. The misunderstandings that surround fistula do not help patients either. I distinctly recall numerous occasions when I had panic attacks in believing my condition had worsened, and only later to find out it wasn't true; or when I thought I healed and only to experience a relapse a few days later. I also wish I knew what I know now - as I believe I may have avoided fistula in the first place. As I tried to learn about fistula, I came across several common myths and facts about fistula. Decoding these myth and facts was a critical step for me. I went from being scared and creeped by fistula, to empowered to confront and address it. My thought process regarding these myth and facts served as the foundation for the self-care regimen I developed for my healing.

As you will find out - while I've developed profound believes on some topics, I am still searching for an answer on others. Although I worked diligently to be medically accurate on many facts, I am not a trained medical professional. Please do forgive me and let me know if you notice any error.

I hope this book will inspire more people, medical professionals in particular, to explore these topics, as we look for a natural cure, or at least, less invasive treatments, of anal fistula together.

Fact: Fistula has nothing to do with the lack of hygiene

Fistula itself can be embarrassingly messy, with the common symptoms including drainage and leakage. The cause of fistula, however, has nothing to do with "messiness". In fact, anal diseases, including commonly occurring hemorrhoids, rarely derive from the lack of hygiene.

Fistula is caused by a bacterial infection that transpires inside the rectum, or sometime, lower intestines. A bacterial infection is a process, in which bacteria invade the body tissues, and white blood cells come to the area to fight off the bacteria.

Our intestinal microflora contains over 400 bacterial species, some of which necessary to keep a healthy stool. Bacteria are normally confined within the bowel "walls" of both intestine and rectal canal. However, if certain spots on the "walls" are compromised or weakened, bacteria can get through and invade the tissues behind the walls. If the bacteria invasion reaches a high level of concentration and our body's first attempt to fight it off does not succeed, a persistent infection will form.

How does compromise occur on the bowel walls/lining to allow bacteria to invade?

First, it can be caused by an inflammation. An inflammation usually manifests as swollenness, redness, a warm or hot feeling, and painfulness. Autoimmune diseases, like Crohn's, cause inflammation of the intestines and rectum by the nature of the illness. People can also develop inflammation in the anal area without any autoimmune diseases. Research has shown stress causes inflammation of body tissues. It can happen anywhere in our body - some areas are more vulnerable than others and it also differs from person to person. This explains why stress gives some people acne breakouts, and others hemorrhoid flare-ups. For those us who suffer ailments of the rear, our ass will thank us if we can keep our stress level at bay!

Two Common Compromises in Anal Canal Lining

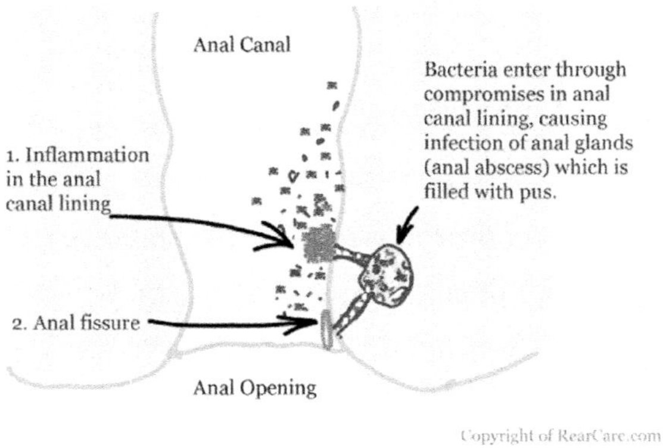

An anal fissure, which is a small tear in the lining of the anal canal and opening, is another common cause for an infection in the anal area. Interestingly, most anal fissures do not lead to an infection despite the fact that there is an actual opening there. Many acute anal fissures heal on their own within 6 weeks without any infection. This is similar to the fact that family members exposed to the same virus don't always all get sick. Besides pure luck, individual's immunity sets us apart as to who gets it, and who does not.

Take-away point-

Fistula has nothing to do with lack of hygiene. Bacterial infection is the reason a fistula develops. Preventing infection would therefore prevent the development of a fistula.

MYTH: You can treat abscess with antibiotic

Antibiotic can treat many bacterial infections effectively, however when it comes to an anal abscess, it depends.

An infection under the inner lining of the rectum can lead to an abscess. What is an abscess? When an infection occurs, our body sends a whole army of white blood cells to the area to fight off bacterial (or viral) invaders. The congested blood cells, dead tissues and bacteria then liquify into a body of pus, walled in like a "balloon". This balloon of pus is called an abscess. As bad a reputation as an abscess has, it actually exists for a noble reason - to confine toxins within its "walls" and prevent them from getting into the blood streams, causing an even more deadly systemic infection. I doubt this explanation will make you love an abscess, but at least "abscess" does have a good excuse.

So why did I mention earlier, the effect of antibiotic on an anal abscess depends? Here's a snippet of what I've learned:

It is believed that blood flow in the rectum area is not sufficient at bringing sufficient levels of antibiotic, which, either taken orally or intravenously, travels through blood streams, to the affected area. Secondly, the abscess wall, which serves as a barrier to stop the toxins from going out, also unfortunately blocks antibiotic from coming in.

Nevertheless, the rule of antibiotic usage has never been a black-and-white one. The first Colon Rectal Surgeon I saw after my abscess diagnosis was adamant, "Antibiotic wouldn't be helpful, and we would just 'wait and see'." While reading patient posts online, I notice patients sometime do receive antibiotic treatment for anal abscesses.

An Urgent Care doctor once told me if strong dosage of antibiotic is given early in the formation of an abscess, where tissues are affected, yet little or no pus is created, an abscess may likely be stopped on its way of formation. If small amount of pus has been generated, it could be absorbed by the surrounding tissues. Therefore, if antibiotic is given in the initial days after the first onset of an infection, it may possibly be effective.

I remember developing an abscess on my chin when I was a teenager. It started from a pimple that got ripped open during a basketball game and a bacterial infection ensued. An abscess was developed and kept growing under the skin. The lower right side of my face was swollen as a result of the infection, to a point my mouth was "pushed" slightly to the left and I couldn't speak clearly for a few days. I was indeed given one week of strong antibiotic via injection. Of course, like a dental abscess, facial abscess presents the risk of spreading the infection into nearby brain tissues.

Regardless, one can't help from asking, "what's the harm with a round of antibiotic, assuming no evidence of chronic misuse is present?" If antibiotic works for early-stage abscesses, why can't it stop infection from worsening and spreading? Maybe, doctors think the danger of antibiotic overuse outweighs the benefit in the case of an anal abscess.

Another thought is - If abscess walls prevent antibiotic from reaching the infection inside the abscess, why can't antibiotic be injected inside an abscess directly.

One online doctor responded that pus has a high acidity that would weaken or diminish the effectiveness of an antibiotic, which is made for a low acidic environment.

A second online doctor expressed an operational concern - injection may cause unintentional puncture of a blood vessel that may release bacteria from the pus into the blood system – leading to a very dangerous condition, "sepsis", that no doctor wants to be accused of causing. With today's modern technology that range from ultrasound to microprobe, exactly how likely this scenario may happen is beyond speculation. However, as one nurse put it, "why would a doctor go out of the norm and try something new like this? After all, if something goes wrong, he or she will be sued out of business."

Take away point –

Antibiotic can be effective on an anal abscess, only when used properly and very early on.

MYTH: How an abscess is drained determines whether a fistula will develop.

When pus continues to collect in the abscess cavity, patients will feel pressure increasing from the pus stretching and suppressing surrounding tissues and nerves. Usually, the pain from the pressure keeps exacerbating until drainage, either on its own or medically, happens.

Our body tissues just can't absorb large amounts of pus fast enough. Once an abscess is well established, let the pus drain out is the only way an abscess can heal.

Exactly how does an anal abscess drain?

First, an anal abscess can drain on its own. This is what happened to me and I do have first-hand experience. Not only that, my abscess drained both internally and externally - two of the possible ways when an abscess drains on its own.

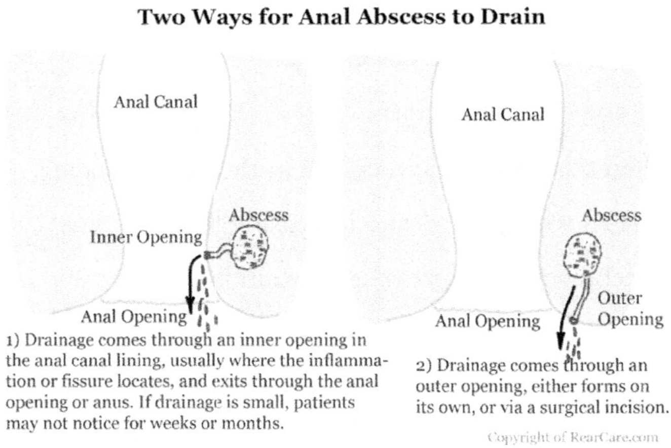

When an abscess was caused by infection through an anal fissure, the fissure tear/opening serves as an inner opening for the abscess. In this scenario, as soon as pus is being built up in the abscess, it will drain back out through the fissure opening. Note - the drainage happens inside the rectum and can be unnoticeable, especially when there's no pain from the pressure or pus build-up. This was exactly how my abscess started and I was not aware of its existence until its diagnosis a couple months later. In retrospect, I did notice spots or stains from drainage.

Eventually one day, a tiny indentation with a hole the size of a pin appeared on the outside surface of where the abscess was underneath. I was sitting in a hot and buzzing Jacuzzi when something felt wrong at my rectum. I immediately got out and looked in a mirror. That's when I first saw the tiny outer opening of the abscess, about 1cm from the anus opening, and right where the abscess was supposed to lie underneath. When pressed with a cotton Q-tip, the tiny hole sent out a few drops of light blood colored pus, along with a very sharp pinching pain.

That's how I learned that an anal abscess can drain on its own both internally and externally. Sometime, internal drainage can go on for months before we notice. Abscess itself is usually not very painful as long as pus could find a way out.

By the way, hot sitz bath is believed to help the development of an outside opening for anal abscesses. In case of extremely painful and well-established abscesses, it is recommended to use hot sitz bath as often as possible to help an outside opening to develop. It sounds crazy to want to a hole to develop on our body, but the alternative, described below, is far worse.

If an anal abscess continues to enlarge due to pus build-up, yet won't pop on its own, the patient can experience a lot of pain. Some describe it as the worst pain in life. It usually requires immediate medical attention not only to relieve pain, but also for the fear that the abscess wall raptures and toxins from the pus get into the bloodstream, which can lead to sepsis. Doctors usually cut a small incision through the outside walls of the anal abscess to allow the pus to release.

However, pus rarely drains up all at one time. Usually, within a few hours to days, a second or more drainage may happen. This is because either some pus is trapped initially, or more pus is generated. I still remember the day when the humongous abscess on my chin popped open on its own, the initial drainage lasted like an eternity - I fondly recall it as if I had a volcanic eruption on my chin. When it finally stopped, the pressure and pain immediately lessened, and the swollenness waned as well. However, the following day a second "eruption" came again, although the drainage was a lot smaller. The relief after that was wonderful. No more drainage followed, and my skin healed the opening quickly, and I got my chin back within a matter of days.

In case more pus needs to drain and the incision opening heals on the outside, which happens more often and faster than we think, it could be devastating to a patient. In that case, a new incision or reopening of the old incision may become necessary.

To prevent the opening from healing too fast, some doctors will stuff medicated gauze through the opening into the cavity of the abscess and leave the end of the gauze out of the opening. This allows drainage to continue through the gauze, while preventing the opening from closing. The procedure needs to be repeated a few times in the first week after an abscess drainage incision was made. Usually without the use of anesthesia, this procedure is claimed as one of the most painful experience for many.

Anal abscess patients live in a lot of unknown. When the abscess is growing, it is not known whether or when it will pop on its own; when the abscess pops or cut open, it is unknown when the drainage is complete and whether the opening will close too soon; and when the drainage is complete, it is unclear if an abscess will turn into a fistula.

When I was first diagnosed with anal abscess, the doctor did mention half abscesses will turn into fistulae. She seemed to indicate the chance of who gets the fistula is pure luck, or bad luck in this case, and patients and doctors have little control over the result.

According to most medical literature, about 50% of anal abscess patients will develop a fistula at the location of the abscess, regardless of how drainage takes place. Just imagine, half of all anal abscesses patients who have suffered tremendous pain from an abscess, and had it properly incised and drained, could still end up with a fistula.

As mentioned earlier, if the draining of an abscess is done effectively, it should eliminate bacteria and other dead cells from gathering inside. This should be the end of an abscess, right? In the case of an anal abscess, it depends. If the compromise in the anal canal lining or the inner opening continues to allow bacteria from our stool enter the abscess cavity, causing repeated infection and more pus, the abscess will re-establish. If the external opening happens to heal up, the abscess will need to drain again, either on its own or through medical incision. The cycle repeats.

In other words, as long as the source of infection still exist, the abscess will persist, and a fistula may ensue.

Take away point –

How an anal abscess is drained does not determine whether a fistula will develop, a recurring infection will.

MYTH: Once you see an outside opening, you have a fistula

Although not all abscesses will turn into fistulae, all anal fistulae start from an abscess. Exactly when an anal abscess turns into a fistula is, in my humble opinion, not a very clearly defined area. To me, this is perhaps the most critical discussion on natural healing of a fistula. It's commonly believed - an abscess can heal on its own, while a fistula rarely does. Too many people however, doctors included, diagnose a fistula too soon. Many commonly diagnosed fistulae are at best "recurring abscesses".

When I first noticed the pin-hole on the outside of my rectum, I was on travel and called my CRS, who immediately told me that's a primary sign of fistula. When I went to see her a few days later, she confirmed that a "fistula" had indeed developed, and surgery was my only option.

As I mentioned earlier, the source of the infection for an anal abscess is from inside the rectum or intestine, where an internal opening continues to let bacteria to enter the abscess. When the abscess repeatedly refills with pus and drains from the outside opening, this becomes a recurring abscess.

Fistula, deriving from its Latin origin, means a pipe, flute. A recurring abscess prevents both the internal and external opening from healing. Scar (hardened) tissue gradually develops around both openings and along the inner walls of the connection. A tunnel with hardened walls is now distinctively developed, connecting the inner rectal canal and the outer skin. This tunnel stays permanently open, even allowing excretion pieces to travel through, hence the word "leakage". This hardened "pipe", now a fully developed fistula, can often be felt under the skin, as it easily stands out from the surrounding soft tissues. The hardened tissue would rarely disappear on its own without medical intervention, such as a surgery. The Indian Kasha Sultra uses a medicated thread to cut through the hardened tissue to allow new tissues to grow and close the fistula tunnel.

Recurring Anal Abcess vs. Anal Fistula

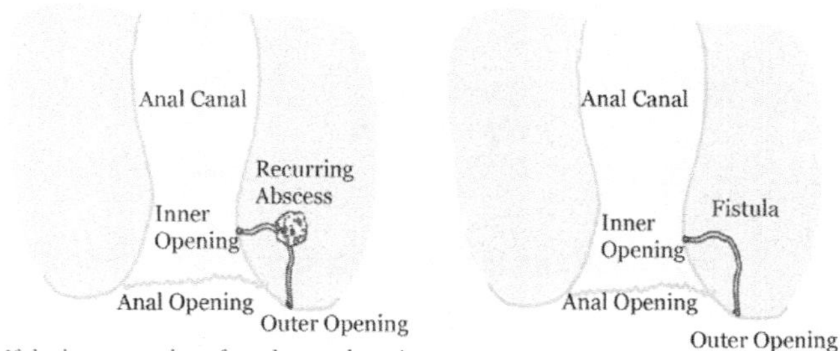

If the inner opening of an abscess doesn't heal and continue to let bacteria in, infection continues, and the abscess will recur, generating more pus which needs to drain from the outer opening.

Over time, recurring abscess will turn into fistula.

My "fistula", which is a common type of "fistula" that regularly calls for a fistulotomy, can, in my opinion, be diagnosed as a recurring abscess. Although a fistulotomy could eliminate an abscess, the possibility does exist that the abscess may heal naturally.

By theory, an abscess, even a recurring one, is an infectious reaction. There is no scar tissue development in an abscess. The treatment of an abscess should focus on infection prevention and drainage. Once the infection stops, the abscess should heal naturally on an otherwise healthy person. As you will find out later, this theory became a reality in my healing.

Take away point –

The sight of an outside opening should not be the gold standard to diagnose a fistula. Recurring abscesses are routinely diagnosed as common fistulae. While patients of recurring abscesses can choose surgery (a fistulotomy, for example, has a success rate of more than 90%), they should also know the possibility of self-healing with proper care.

MYTH: Fistula disappears after it heals.

I was always curious how fistula heals naturally. With surgery, such as a fistulotomy (the simplest of all fistula surgeries), the fistula is cut open, hard tissues that forms the fistula tube is scraped out, new tissue grows and fills the gap. A scar is what would remain after the wound heals. What about natural healing then? Will the entire fistula disappear?

As I've discovered with my own experience, it's not quite how I thought it would heal. When the CRS declared that my fistula closed on its own, the outer opening was still there and visible – an identifying symptom of fistula. Therefore, I had no reason to speculate that the fistula healed.

To confirm his diagnosis, the CRS did an anoscopy and informed me that the inner opening had healed. Next, he put a probe, a flexible needle, into the outer opening. After repeated poking, he said it had closed inside.

Reflectively speaking, this all makes sense. The inner opening has to close to stop further infection. Once the infection stops, the tunnel of the fistula collapses. The outer opening looks like a tiny pit. If you look up "preauricular sinus or fistula", the healed outer opening looks exactly like that. I was born with two preauricular sinus or fistula on my ears, both asymptomatic all my life.

Recurring abscess / Fistula Healing

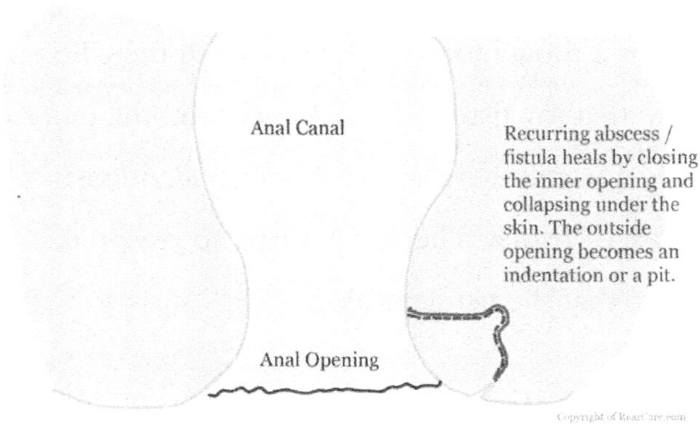

At some point when a recurring abscess turns into a

fistula, the cavity/tunnel wall turns into a hardening tissue. This hardening tissue is what people call "a hard pipe" that can be felt under skin. The window of natural healing most likely comes before this hardening tissue develops. I believe I took the right actions before the hardening tissue developed.

The healed abscess will continue to remain a vulnerability for years. For example, years after the abscess healed on my chin, I had, from time to time, felt a small bean-shaped lump where the abscess was. It usually resolved on its own after a few days. Now I don't feel any residue of an abscess there at all. Abscess natural healing is a long-term process. The key from my experience is "Never to take our body for granted any more. Tune in to our body and address pains and discomforts early on. Over time, our body will make the rectification needed."

Take away point -

Fistula does not just disappear. Fistula natural healing is not an overnight miracle. The goal of natural healing is to keep the fistula "closed", "dormant", and "asymptomatic" for the rest of our life.

4. Developing My Healing Regimen

After walking through my thought process, now let's dive right in how I practiced my self-care regimen, which led to my natural healing.

After I was given the verdict that fistula won't heal on its own and I will need a fistulotomy sooner or later, I told the doctor I wanted to wait a little to make a decision.

I had a good reason to stay away from any surgery at that time. My whole ordeal started from a hemorrhoidectomy at the end of 2016. The pain after the surgery was the worst in my life. Although the surgical incision did heal a few weeks later, I had developed a chronic fissure a couple months after the surgery, and the fissure then led to an infection which developed into an abscess. After 5 months, the abscess developed an outside opening, hence the fistula diagnosis. At the time of the fistula diagnosis, I was still in pain from the fissure and it had only been 8 months since the hemorrhoidectomy. Another surgery was the last thing on my mind.

My resistance to another surgery therefore turned into a motivation to find an alternative. In addition, by the time my fistula was diagnosed, I had developed a whole set of daily regimen to manage and care for my symptoms. I had done a significant amount of research about rectal ailments.

I examined my situation rationally. I knew I had a very healthy diet; I exercised regularly; my BM was at the most optimal condition as humanly possible; I bathed immediately after each BM; and I practiced warm sitz bath every night. I knew I was doing everything right. I remember saying to myself, if I had taken such good care of myself years before, I probably would have cured my not-so-severe hemorrhoids and avoided the hemorrhoidectomy in the first place.

The first thing I did after noticing the outside opening of the fistula and the small amount of pus coming out of it was to keep the area clean at all times and apply a small amount of Neosporin (anti-biotic cream) at the outside opening two times a day. The Neosporin would take care of the infection immediately. Pus would stop the next day.

However, a few days later, small amounts of pus would reappear. After the application of Neosporin, the fistula would fall in a slumber for a few more days. My doctor had indicated the inner opening of the fistula is where I had the fissure. Apparently, my fissure not only did not heal, it had become chronic, leaving an opening for bacteria from the stool to invade in.

Since Neosporin did such a good job at eliminating

infection from outside, I thought if I could apply Neosporin inside my rectum, wouldn't that do the trick? My fissure, or the inner opening, was very close to the anal opening, approximately 1cm. I was told this is called a "low" fistula, meaning it is close to the anal opening, involving little sphincter muscle, and is a perfect "candidate" for fistulotomy.

Neosporin specifies that it is for external use only. I hesitated, before I decided that 1cm inside the rectum is very close to being "external". Of course, I can't possibly be sure how exactly to apply any medicine on top of the inner opening of a fistula. I just reassured myself that if I could get the Neosporin in the vicinity of the inner opening, that should be more beneficial than none.

Infection usually occurs during or after a BM, when the bacteria-ridden stool passes the inner opening of a fistula. Neosporin is best to be applied immediately after a BM. To be more effective, I bathed after each BM and made sure the exterior was completely clean. Next, I used Vaseline covered Q-tips to clean the inside just enough until there was no stool left on the Q-tips (yes, I did run through hundreds or maybe thousands of Q-tips). Then I send in a small amount of Neosporin and finished up by applying Neosporin over the outside opening.

Of course, all of this is done with the help of a mirror. If you still find this idea of "checking our bum with a mirror" mentally challenging to accept, either your suffering is not bad enough or you are not desperate enough. I was at a point where I would do anything to get my normal life back, hopefully without another surgery. No social taboo or embarrassment would have a place in my way of healing.

Shortly after I started this ritual, my infection started to become less frequent. It went from skipping one week without drainage, to two weeks, to a month. It was amazing!

I thought I was healing well. Then one day after a bout of diarrhea (three times a day), I felt some tenderness at the fistula spot. I pressed a Q-tip at the outside opening. When I lifted it up, I saw a familiar reddish spot at the tip of the Q-tip. I knew the infection was back and so was the pus. I knew diarrhea made it hard to keep clean inside. I needed a better way of keeping the inside clean after a BM.

Not too long prior to this new infection, I had come across an online post about some patients in China practice douching to keep inside clean. Thinking I should give it a try, I ordered a rectal enema douche.

To be completely honest, this idea was harder to implement than I thought. When I saw the rectal enema douche, I did not think I could manage to put the enema's nozzle in, even though the diameter of the nozzle was about half of my pinkie. I always had a scary experience with an enema in the past. This new "tool" seemed too much a hurdle to overcome. I had left the douche in the closet for weeks.

Now under this new round of infection, I knew the only thing I hadn't tried was the douche. After a BM one morning, I covered the douche nozzle with a layer of Vaseline. The sliding in was really easy. Squirting water in was a bit strange, but tolerable. I used lukewarm water to lessen the shock cold water may have caused inside my rectum. For the initial days of my douching, I even used saline water (by melting some salt in lukewarm water). I used just lukewarm water afterwards.

The most challenging, or scary part, to me was when the water came back out, as it could cause the most pain if the water happens to irritate the fissure tear/inner opening of the fistula. Although I had to say, the fear probably outweighed the actual pain, which was usually transient in a split of a second.

Each douche used about 5 oz of water. If water looked contaminated on the way out, I would repeat until it become fairly clear. Usually 2~3 douches would do. I would douche every morning after each BM. I clean myself in shower afterwards. I finished everything by applying Neosporin on the outside and inside as I did before.

Once I got a hang of it, my morning bathroom routine took about half an hour. When I emerged from the bathroom, I literally felt like a new person - clean inside and out!

In the next four months, I only had two small infections. Both times I had suffered diarrhea, or multiple BMs a day, and did not get to sanitize immediately after.

I started very carefully to stay away from food that would trigger a diarrhea. I also managed to sanitize immediately after a BM even I could not get back home quickly. I would wipe clean with disinfectant wet wipes and apply Neosporin on the outside right away (and inside if I had Q-tips and Vaseline at hand). And I would find a way to head home early and conduct a proper douche.

This routine went on for months and months. I did skip applying Neosporin eventually and only used it occasionally (trying to avoid resistance to antibiotics).

I kept on douching each and every day.

When I went to see the doctor who declared my healing, I had practiced douching for a little less than one year. The doctor did an anoscope and pointed out the inner opening of the fistula has closed. There is still a small indented hole from the outside. When he put a probe into the outside opening, the probe was obstructed and wouldn't go through – one can only imagine that new tissue had grown and filled the inside of the fistula.

I stopped douching after that, knowing there isn't an inner opening any more. I am letting the newly healed inner lining to do the job at keeping bacteria from getting in.

Remember the abscess I had on my chin when I was teenager. I remember I would feel the cavity (lump) of the abscess for many years to come. Sometimes, under stress, I may even feel an inflammation (enlarged lump) there again. It never developed into an abscess again. However, it actually took years before I can no longer feel the abscess any more. So I know anal abscess will behave the same way, and I am committed to do my best not to give it any chance to revive.

If you are interested in more details of how I did my day-to-day healing regimen, you can continue to read the next section.

5. A Close Look at My Healing Regimen

My self-healing regimen consisted of four essential elements:

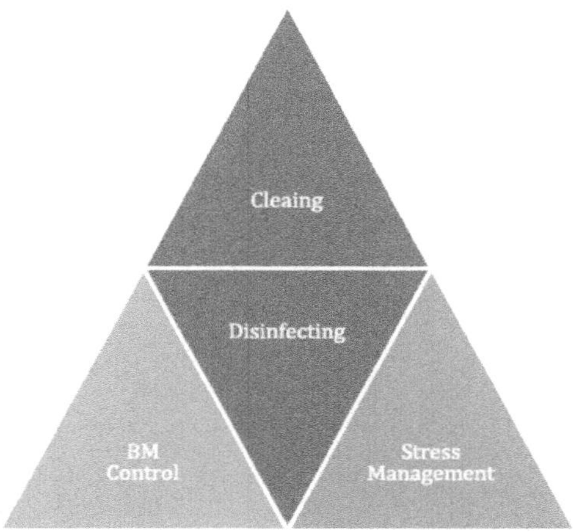

Cleaning - Stop bacteria from entering into the body tissues - by keeping the inner and outer openings clean to ensure no contamination gets in

Disinfecting - Use topical antibiotics both on the outer and inner openings to eliminate bacterial infection

BM Control - Manage an optimal BM schedule that features one easy/non-straining BM a day at relatively the same time

Stress Management - Manage life stress whenever necessary to avoid stress-derived inflammation.

Cleaning

It is essential to clean the outside and inside of the abscess/fistula openings after each and every bowel movement, to prevent bacteria contained in the excrete from invading through the fistula/abscess opening.

This process should be executed religiously following each BM, including after each diarrhea, even if there are multiple a day. Although it only occurred to me a few times, I definitely noticed loose stool was more likely to induce infection. Liquid loose stool can more easily enter through the fistula/abscess opening. As a result, diarrhea should be avoided at all times, if possible. I consciously stayed away from food that may trigger diarrhea. However, for a patient with Crohn's, controlling diarrhea may not be as easy. One Crohn patient said that after trying different approaches, he successfully controlled diarrhea by taking low dosage of Imodium, an antidiarrheal medicine. As a result of reduced diarrhea, his fistula flare ups also significantly reduced. If you suffer frequent diarrhea, please explore, with the help of your doctor, possible ways to prevent diarrhea. In my experience, this step is essential in healing and controlling fistula symptoms.

The process to clean inside a rectum takes some trial and error. But ultimately it is to find a way that works for you. As I mentioned earlier, I practice douching to clean the inside and only stopped after the doctor declared the inside opening had healed completely. I personally used a douche I purchased on Amazon. There are many reviews and Q&A about its usage. So, I don't need to go into too much detail. Douching was the last step I added to my daily healing regimen and probably the final step that sealed my healing. I absolutely stand by its significance. If you think the idea of douching scary, I want to assure you - If I can do it, you can. You see - I used to be horrified by the thought of an enema. Douching was completely out of the question for me. It took me a long time to accept the idea of douching, and another few more weeks to work up the courage to actually act on it. Now knowing its benefit, I wish I had started douching earlier - it could have made my healing a lot sooner.

When it comes to private matters such as "care for one's rear", I notice learning the terminology does not mean knowing how. Bathroom affairs are extremely private matters. Even family members who share the same roof may not necessarily know each other's bathroom habits. Most people have heard of douching, yet doing it on your own can be completely foreign and daunting!

Although you are free to explore a way that works best for you, it is hard to know what's best if you have no clue how to even start. What I did was to check out online posts and YouTube videos on douching and developed my own method. I have to say it worked darn well for me! I am here to share this extremely personal experience and detailed steps, hoping to give you a kick start.

Get into a warm shower after a BM. Rinse the outside of the anus area thoroughly, including the outside opening of a fistula/abscess. Warm water also relaxes the sphincter muscles. Please note - I did my entire douche while the shower is running on me. I found it relaxing and calming.

In a plastic cup, put in one teaspoon of Epsom salt. This step is optional. I used Epsom salt water, because of its perceived healing effect. Fill up the cup with warm shower water to about one cup. Wait until Epsom salt dilutes. Make sure water is not too hot to the touch.

Squeeze air out of douche ball and absorb Epsom salt water into douche ball. Cover Douche snout with one teaspoonful of Vaseline as lubricant.

Lift up one leg and rest that foot on a stool. Knee should be above hip for easier access. Use both hands, one in the front as a guide, and one in the back holding the douche ball. The guiding hand helps the snout to locate the anus opening, and gently send the snout in. I usually try to get one inch (3cm) of the snout in. I believe it was sufficient as the inside opening of my fistula was fairly close to the anus opening.

Gently squeeze water into rectum. I did somewhere

between ½ and one full cup of water each time. Keep squeezing the douche ball as you gently pull out the snout with the guiding hand. If you release douche ball while the snout is still inside your rectum, you would suck in the now contaminated water back in the douche ball. This is ok if you don't mind cleaning the inside of the douche thoroughly later.

Put both feet on the floor. Either sit on a toilet or on a portable potty/bucket in the shower, and let the water run out from your rectum. It is common to have some loose stool coming out with the first douche.

I usually repeat douching one or two more times. When the exiting water looks relatively clear, the cleaning process is now over."

Disinfecting

At this step, I use common over-the-counter disinfectant, such as Neosporin to kill any residue bacteria that are probably lingering around the outside and inside fistula/abscess opening. Below is how I did it:

Again, lift up one leg on a stool. Put a small mirror and flashlight on the stool and facing your bottom. This allows me to monitor the process by looking into the reflection of the mirror.
Use a Q-tip to dry the outside opening of a fistula/abscess. Cover another Q-tip with Vaseline first, and then a small pea sized Neosporin. Apply Neosporin to the outside fistula/abscess opening. Toss the Q-tip.

Prepare another Q-tip with Vaseline first and then Neosporin. Send Neosporin into the anus. Make sure to push most of the Neosporin in, especially onto the walls where the inside opening locates. This completes the disinfecting step. Vaseline serves as lubricant and wound healer.

BM Control

As I mentioned earlier, it is essential to keep an optimal BM routine. The "Cleaning" and "Disinfecting", no matter how often, may not keep up with risks caused by frequent diarrhea, and/or straining during BMs. I am a firm believer that everybody's BM routine can be improved through diet, regardless of where you stand on the optimal BM spectrum. The ideal BM routine should include one easy BM once a day and at around the same time. If that's not where you are right now, you should first and for most, focus on improving it immediately. There's a lot of useful information online about constipation and diarrhea control. Patients with IBS, Chron's shouldn't give up either. Everyone has room to improve.

For me, my fistula/abscess was the result of a fissure, which was a rare complication from a hemorrhoidectomy (a surgical procedure to remove external hemorrhoids). My hemorrhoids were the result of years of strained BMs. I was never badly constipated, yet chronic straining took a toll.

After the hemorrhoidectomy, I made the following dietary changes to achieve the optimal BM routine:

One of the revolutionary discoveries I had in my healing was how little water I was drinking before. When the doctor asked me to keep track of how much water I was drinking, to my dismay, I found my daily water intake was at most at half of the recommended 8-glass level. It just never occurred to me to check my daily water intake.

Without enough water consumption, there won't be enough moisture in the stool – pretty straight forward. The water contained in fruits, veggies and soup should not factor in the daily measurement. If you experience constipation or straining, check your water intake first.

I also find out drinking 8 glasses of pure water is not easy at the beginning. It is a habit that I had to push myself to learn and to be accustomed.

I now start my day with two glasses of water. On cold days, I drink warm water. I find drinking warm water in the morning relaxes my digestive system and gets the bowel moving.

I mentioned about changing diet drastically to achieve optimal BM. How drastic exactly? In my case, I went all vegetable. All vegetable is one step more restrictive than all plant. Vegetables, especially green leafy ones, have soft and long non-soluble fibre, which produces the desirable soft and long stools. I also opt not to eat any kinds of grains, especially the refined and bleached type, which is known to cause bulky stools. Even whole grain products, such as whole wheat, if taken without enough water, can result in bulky stools. Interestingly, this grain-less diet has already been well researched and documented in the dietary literature, and is named Paleo Diet. You can read all about it. Paleo diet advocates believe human bodies are not wired properly to process food created after the Palaeolithic period, including grains which were only mass produced after farming was practiced. I eat yogurt, eggs, and small amount of chicken and fish to get the protein my body needs. To facilitate and regulate the process, I also take MiraLAX daily.

After practicing the above measures, my BM routine improved within a couple of days. Once my BM was on its optimal track for an extended period, I, a bread lover, started to introduce some grain-based food, about 25% into my total diet. I make sure to eat grain-based food with pretty of water and chew thoroughly. I continued to avoid rice. I also reduced MiraLAX to half of its daily dosage.

As mentioned earlier, diarrhea is more threatening to fistula/abscess, as the liquid stool can more easily enter the internal openings. Constipation should also be strictly avoided as inflammation caused by straining can worsen fistula and abscess symptoms.

Stress Management

As my body has demonstrated in the last two years, once an anal abscess or fistula develops, it becomes a weakest link of the body. Whenever stress strikes, your body's immunity system weakens, the abscess or fistula area becomes more susceptible to inflammation and/or infections. This has happened to me multiple times and I cannot ignore its significance. Patients with abscess/fistula need to be mindful of the impact of stress and manage stress levels accordingly and don't let stress become your enemy at healing.

I know stress can sneak into our life sometimes without us knowing. Almost every time this happened, there were signs early on - a sore throat, a low pain or pressure in the anal area, but I was ignoring it, until infection symptoms flared up badly. I believe it is essential fistula/abscess patients tune in their bodies attentively, know what is normal, pick out stress signals and learn to de-stress regardless of the situations.

About 10 months after the doctor declared "my fistula had healed", I went through a bout of stressful days and ignored my dietary routines. I noticed a dull pain at the anus opening. I was too distracted to pay attention. By the fourth day, the pain was getting worse. I immediately went for a sitz bath and felt the anus area was swollen and painful to touch. My fistula outer opening, which had been just a pit by then, was very tender to touch. Almost to my despair, I felt a pea size of lump underneath. There was nothing visible from the outside and no drainage. The lump, however, alarmed me that it could be an abscess again. The next day I scheduled an appointment with the same doctor who declared my healing, but the appointment was not until one week away. As you probably can relate, I lived several panicky days.

Fortunately, I was a veteran at self-care already. I practiced warm sitz bath whenever I could, mindfully distracted myself from the stressful situation, returned back to optimal diet, etc. My body reacted to these measured rather quickly. On the third day after I practiced my self-care ritual, I remember rising from bed feeling significantly less pain. I knew at that moment I should be ok. I am pretty sure the pea-sized lump was the old abscess trying to redevelop and my effective measures stopped it from happening. I am quite thrilled that my body fended off a potential flare-up of pain and suffering. This incident let me realize my bottom is perhaps the weakest link in my body - it will easily comprise when stresses hits. Everybody has one or a couple weakest links in their body where problems tend to occur when you are under the weather, be it a sore throat, stuffy nose, pimples, headache, etc. For fistula/abscess patients, it's our bottom.

If your fistula/abscess indeed heals like mine, it is very important to take care of your body physically and mentally, and don't let stress build up. For years after the abscess in my chin healed which I had when I was a colleague student, I could, from time to time, feel a small lump under the skin where the abscess was. Often when I was under the weather, the lump got a bit bigger. Once I felt better, the lump shrank to nearly nothing. This lasted many years before it perpetually disappeared. It is probably safe to assume anal abscess would behave in the same way. Proper self-care is essential at preventing the abscess from coming back.

6. My Fistula-Healing Essentials

Readers are usually curious about the products I used in my healing. As I mentioned before, there's no magic tool or medicine here. Instead, everything I used was just inexpensive and common items you can easily find. Below is a list of essential products I used in my healing. For more information on these products, please visit http://rearcare.com/my-fistula-anal-abscess-healing-essentials/

- Neosporin
- Vaseline
- Q-tips
- Douche
- Epsom salt

- Flushable wipes
- Portable Putty
- MiraLAX
- Bidet

7. Q&A with Fellow Patients

I want to share some of my communications with fellow patients, hoping these conversations might help you in some ways. When it comes to anal illnesses, it is critical we take ownership and be the best advocate for ourselves. We have to, because nobody else, even the doctors (especially they are not with us 24/7), can really feel what we feel or even take a good look at our wound(s) down there. While I encourage everyone to keep communicating with your doctor, it is absolutely critical that every patient be educated and understand the fundamentals of the anal anatomy and the causes of anal dysfunctions. Asking questions is one big part of learning about and managing this illness.

1. *How long should I practice the regimen? - I got an anal abscess and my family doctor told me that I may need to get incision for drainage. When I learned about the probability to get fistula after an incision, I started to look for some natural healing methods and came upon your book. I am practicing all the steps in your regimen. I have done that in the last 7 days and the size of the abscess has extremely reduced. My question is "how long should I practice disinfection?"* (M, Canada)

Answer: I stopped applying Neosporin to disinfect when I didn't feel any pain, discomfort, nor did I see any drainage. After that, I would continue to clean, but only used Neosporin occasionally when I felt some pain or discomfort, which is a sign that the infection is brewing for a comeback. Using disinfectants at these occasions keeps the recurring infection at bay. It's never a good idea to overuse any medicine, including over-the-counter disinfectant/antibiotic, like Neosporin. As I mentioned earlier in the book, "cleaning" alone can prevent recurring infection. Neosporin is applied to address ongoing infection. It shouldn't be used for prevention on a regular basis.

2. *Can I use an alternative to Neosporin?*

Answer: Several fellow patients have brought up a few different replacements of Neosporin based on where they are residing and what's available to them. I unfortunately don't have the resources to test any of them personally. I will share the names of these alternatives with you as a reference in case you are wondering: Medihoney (in UK), Propsporin (in Canada), Sudocrem (India), and Bacitracin.

I have learned a few interesting facts of antibiotic creams. For example, some antibiotic cream only addresses one type of bacteria (Neosporin does contain a combination of antibiotics and therefore offers a broader antibiotic coverage). While antibiotics kill bacteria, antiseptics are best for helping clean and slow the growth of bacteria. I personally didn't try antiseptics. I encourage you to know what you are using and try different solutions, if possible, to find what works best for you.

3. *Should I take any supplement? - I'm wondering if you took any supplements for your healing? I've been taking some supplements to boost my immunity like cows colostrum and herbal supplement called Intra. Taking the supplements is helping tremendously but I've been taking them for the last 3 months and I don't want my immune system to become too dependent on them should there be any long term effect of using them daily.* (L, U.S.)

Answer: Supplement and particular diets are not something I covered much in my book, mostly because there are some good resources out there on the internet available to everyone. Although I'm not against taking any supplement, I haven't taken any supplement in particular for my healing. Besides a balanced diet, physical exercises are always helpful to increase blood flow into the anal area and facilitate the healing.

4. *How long did it take to heal? – Now it seems my*

abscess is getting better, but not fully recovered. I still have small amounts of pus coming out daily, usually in the evening. How long do I have to do this until I don't have any more pus forming up? Months? Years? (J, Thailand)

Answer: My healing trajectory started like a rollercoaster, where I was ecstatic when my drainage or pus went down, or even stopped, and only to find the pus coming back a few days later. Remember, I was not practicing the cleaning/disinfecting regimen consistently at the beginning, because I was still trying to figure out what worked, and what didn't. As my cleaning and disinfecting practice became more regular, my overall symptoms started to fall, even though it was not a straight line of decline (as seen in the My Healing Trajectory chart below) at first. It was pretty clear to me back then that I was heading toward "getting better". Eventually, my drainage or discomfort disappeared completely for months. That's when I went back to see the doctor and heard the words that my fistula "had closed on its own". After that, I only practiced disinfecting occasionally when I felt discomfort. I continued to clean until another follow-up visit with the doctor 8 months later to confirm that the fistula remained closed.

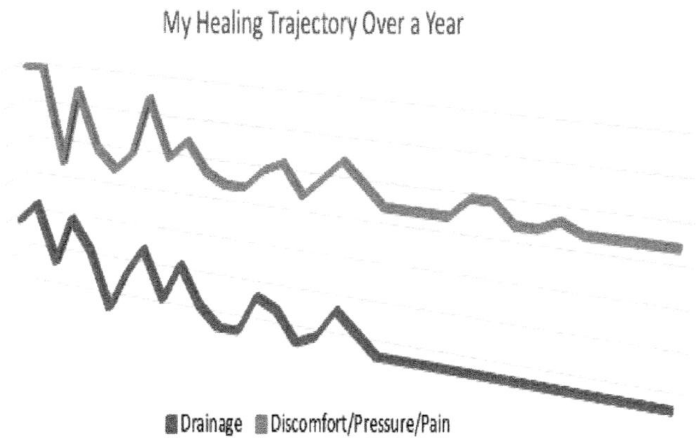

Everybody's healing trajectory will be different, of course. It won't be a quick fix for most. If this method works for you, you should feel signs of getting better very quickly, even though you are not completely healed yet. As anal fistula patients know very well, while some fistulae keep a pretty consistent profile of symptoms including minimal daily draining, some very active fistulae can branch off and worsen very quickly. Before I knew I would eventually heal from the fistula, I told myself that at least what I was doing kept my symptoms from getting worse and bought me time to consider if I would eventually need a surgery.

5. *Were you ever worried that by foregoing/ delaying surgery there was a risk of the fistula spreading and becoming more complex?* (P, India)

Answer: Of course. I worried very much at the beginning (before I knew I would heal eventually), especially on days when I felt my symptoms were a bit worse. However, on the most part, I could tell my symptoms were getting better - I was feeling less and less pain, my drainage reduced or stopped (for a couple days at the beginning, then for an entire week, then more weeks, and finally months…) What you asked is a very real question - my hindsight advice is that our body will tell us if we are getting better or not.

6. *I was diagnosed with Fistula in Dec 2020. The history is similar to yours. Fissure in 2018 and then followed by abscess and then Fistula. In the cleaning process, I observed*

some bleeding. When I put the Q-tip with the vaseline and Neosporin I observed blood in the bud when I took it out. I just wanted to check with you is it possible that I might have hurt the internal opening further which might have caused the bleeding? (A, India)

Answer: Most likely, your bleeding comes from the fissure. I have experienced this many times – I actually noticed blood quite often at the beginning. Bleeding is a common symptom of a fissure. You will know because there is pain/discomfort during BM. You can use a lubricated (like Vaseline coated) Q-tip to probe after a BM. If there is blood, your bleeding comes from the fissure wound. You can choose to wait a few days until the fissure pain comes down. Or you can use the Vaseline coated Q-tip to start cleaning, since this is less irritating. If I had a painful BM and didn't want to further disturb my wound, I would switch to the Q-tip method to avoid any further irritation. Hope this helps. Anal fissure is another tenacious battle for patients like you and me. It's important you distinguish the symptoms between a fissure and fistula though, so you can address them more accordingly.

7. *I notice Neosporin's instruction indicates that it can't be used longer than 2 weeks. How long did you use Neosporin as disinfectant?* (Y, Indonesia)

Answer: The concern of using "Neosporin" for too long is two folds: (1) Neosporin kills both good and bad bacteria. Using it for a long time can change the natural bacterial composition. Our body needs good bacteria for different purposes. For example, good bacteria are important for proper digestion in our digestive track. We have good bacteria even our mouths. Applying Neosporin at the very end of the anal canal, where no digestion is taking place, shouldn't be a big concern in my opinion. (2) Using Neosporin too long may cause antibiotic-resistance in bacteria. This can be a real concern, although I never had any issues even though I used Neosporin on and off for months. Two things I did may be helpful for you to know - First, I only used a small amount (my pinkie fingernail size or less) once a day to cover fistula's small openings; secondly, I did stop from time to time when I didn't have any of the symptoms, such as pain and pus (I would only practice cleaning).

8. *The Neosporin's package mentions it is for external application only. Can you confirm if this is the ointment you used?* (R, India)

Answer: Neosporin does indicate for external application only. I decided to take some measured risk throughout this process, including applying some Neosporin at the very end of my rectum. You will have to make the decision yourself. You can always start by applying on the outside/external opening first, as I did, and see if your body responds positively - just a suggestion. I've also learned that some people have minor allergic reactions to Neosporin. It is always a good practice to try on your external skin first to see if there's any redness or discomfort.

9. *As I check online regarding regular douching, many sites warn against frequent douching, i.e. more than 2-3 times a week, as there is danger of causing structural damage?* (F, Spain)

Answer: For me - each douching lasts seconds (30seconds), because I literally let water out seconds after I squirt it in. The squirting should be gentle enough as never to cause any pain. Lukewarm water only, not hot. my douching also only just focused on the lower end of the rectum where the inner opening is. Pat outside dry when done.

This might change the bacteria/chemical mix in the rectum a bit. But for 30 seconds to 1 minute a day, I doubt it is too bad. Again, I never had any issue. I think if something is not right, our body will tell us before it gets bad. In that case, stop or reduce immediately.

10. *Can I also check how far in, from the outside of the rectum were you applying the antibiotic and Vaseline? Had you somehow located the inner opening?* (F, Spain)

Answer: I put Antibiotic 1cm in, definitely less than 2cm. My inner opening was where I had a fissure and it is pretty close to the rectum opening, according to my doctor. I do think it's extremely important to have some idea of where your inner opening is, ideally with the help of a doctor. In my case, the pain from the fissure (when I used a Q-tip to probe) also helped me locate the inner opening. Admittedly, I could never be too precise when I tried to apply antibiotic. I think to apply it in the vicinity is good enough as it will kill bacteria in the area.

I do think if the inner opening is too far in, it would be difficult to reach with antibiotic. In that case, let's just hope douching/cleaning (maybe with Epsom salt water) and antibiotic on the outside can help. Again, your body will tell you if it works.

If you have additional questions and suggestions, please email me at **rearcare.regimen@gmail.com**.

If you have healed, please let me know as well. Let's all contribute to finding and defining a natural cure for this condition.

8. Acknowledgement

I thank hundreds of patients who shared their experience. Many had made a significant impact on my life, especially my healing. I hope my contribution, either via www.RearCare.com or this book, benefit many as well.

I thank my family (both by blood and by law) for providing me the understanding and support I dearly needed and relied upon to practice the self-care regimen during my healing. I thank my parents' optimism and unconditional love, to form who I am and my resilience to life's obstacles.

I thank you, the reader, for investing in this book and

for supporting what I do for the Rear Care community. If you have any questions or suggestions, please email me at rearcare.regimen@gmail.com. I actually learn a lot from my readers like you through the Q&A process and will turn around to educate others.

Please also consider give this book a positive review and good rating to let me know I am doing a good job helping our community.
Lastly, I hope this book sends you the positive vibes you need to head to your healing!

.

9. About the Author

Penni X. W. is a university research fellow, who resides in northern America. Her research focus is on learning design and technologies. She has contributed to the production of many educational products.

Printed in Great Britain
by Amazon

47645043R00051